COMING
2
AMERICA

JOHN AKINYEMI

This is the story of Agnes Ndungwa Akinyemi, my beloved wife, an incredible woman, the Rock of my life and a great blessing to the entire extended families, namely the AKINYEMI, SOREMEKUN, MUTHIANI and MUSAU families.

My first order of business is to determine what title I am going to give to this biography. Here are the thoughts that came to my mind:

1. GOING TO AMERICA I didn't want to title it "COMING TO AMERICA", for fear of infringing on proprietary copyright laws on Eddie Murphy's movie by that title.

2. FROM NOBODY TO SOMEBODY: ONLY IN AMERICA. Either of these two will do it, I said to myself. The bookcover will include her High School graduation photo at age 18 followed by the following words: "A narrative story of a 15 year-old African girl, Agnes Akinyemi's sojourn in America.

PREFACE

Agnes had a great life. This is a story of that great life. I had planned to write her biography and she had helped me tell it in her own words as tellingly as she could and as many times as she did when she was still alive and enjoyed her full mental faculty. She had done this in front of her family when they gave her a "surprise visit" in 2018, and subsequent visits culminating in May, 2021, exactly one month prior to the day she passed on June 2021. Three of her nieces, Kalekje, Katunge, and Mutheo spent a week with her, prayed with and for her, sang and danced with her, and helped with the chores of taking care of a loved one with dementia, etc. Their visit, which ended up as their "last visit" was truly a testimony to a remark I had made five or so years ago: "Don't send a truck-load of flowers when I die, let me smell them when I'm alive and well".

I faced the "challenge" most authors and biographers face: namely selection. Seemingly not enough time or space to tell it all. I was determined to write a single volume of reasonable length. Mine is the story of an African girl, more precisely a fifteen year old Kenya- born girl who was "destined" to come to America from a family of limited means in Kangundo District. That girl, at 15 years of age, somehow ended up working at the Clinical Pathology Department at the National Institutes of Health, Bethesda, Maryland, USA, graduating with a Master of Science degree in

Microbiology from "the" premier Historically Black University, HBU, "Howard University", Washington DC., working towards earning a PhD in Microbiology at the University of Maryland in Baltimore County (UMBC), and then working for, and retiring from, the United States Department of Army, Aberdeen Proving Ground, Maryland as a Microbiologist for 24 years! It is a story of hard work; a story of "good luck". It is a story of occasional hardship, but undaunted perseverance. It is a story that once you are at the bottom of a ladder, there's nowhere else to go but up! It is a story of mostly "blessed" times. It is a story about the people who helped make Agnes what she was for 76 years of her life. It is a story of her many nieces, including Kakekje, Katunge, Mutheo, Mikki, Mira, her sister-in-law, Salome, and Agnes's younger brother, Jackson Maingi Muthiani, and many other family members, and friends not listed in this biography because of the challenge I referred to earlier, namely, contend with selection. The list is long, of who benefitted from opportunities created by their aunt, "matriach of the family", and brother who followed her. It is a story that will benefit even the yet-to-be born who will follow. It is a story of faith: faith in God, faith in herself, and faith in America. It is a story that convinces me that if I had been sick the way she was, she would take care of me the same way I did. I know this without any shadow of doubt in my mind. Best of all, it is a "love story": love of family, love of friends, love of her native country, Kenya, and love of this great Nation, America. In the words of the late United States Supreme Court's Chief Justice, Judge Greenberg, "It is a story that only could have happened in America.", for America is the ONLY country in the world, where a "nobody can become a "somebody" if that "nobody" is willing to work hard. May God Bless the USA!

This was the photo of Agnes's graduation from
Madona High School in 1964

I am JOHN A. AKINYEMI. Agnes always delighed in introducing me to people with this favorite phrase "this is JOHN AKINYEMI, my husband" with slight emphasis and a.drawl on the word "husband" "I am blessed with this Yoruba man, a good man, from Nigeria", she would add. It is no wonder we have a mutual feeling in this regard. I am blessed I married you, Agnes, in 1971, the best Kikamba woman in the world," I would add. Without a doubt, we are a "super blessed" couple. Somebody once said to me especially when you have known each other since 1964. To come to think of it, that is over five decades ago! Half a Century! That by itself is a special blessing! We got to a point in our lives where either one of us could finish the thoughts on each other's minds, and be right on-the-button! After she reached age 72 and her memory began to fail, I could hear her "sound of silence." Time and time again when I looked at her, I could hear her sound of silence. She "dazzled me" with her sparkling, beautiful white teeth (all her natural teeth, by the way), and great smiles. She didn't need to move her lips or open her mouth, I hear her voice of silence!. When she said "give me your hand, John, I know she was telling me something very important!. I remember one time when she was having difficulty voiding urine, She said John, please help me, I am having trouble". I am right here with you, honey, I said, but I cannot help you with my organ; I am a male" As I write this incredible story of Agnes's life, I give glory and honor to GOD because GOD made Agnes "The Rock" of my life. And I am eternally thankful to Him.

Isn't it amazing that a young lady from MACHAKOS, KANGUNDO, KENYA, EAST AFRICA, and a young Yoruba man, from ABEOKUTA, NIGERIA, WEST AFRICA, would meet, not in Central Africa, but iin the cold State of Illinois, USA?

Yes, that's right. Our paths. crossed in 1964. Agnes was admitted to, and started as a freshman student at Aurora college Aurora Illinois. I was a sophomore student then.

The story of how we met is very interesting. A foreign student, Zoheir Kashoo, from Syria, my college mate, had told me: "John, do you know there's an African girl in town? "No way!, I said. However, I decided to check it out! Yes, indeed Zoheir was right. There was an African girl in Aurora Town. I found out she was living with a White American family, Vernon and Anne Pettit. I found out their names in the Yellow Pages of the telephone. I found their address. 200 block of Randall Rd. This is "exciting" I said to myself. 211 Randal Rd is not too far from the college campus. "I can even walk there However, for safety sake, I decided against walking. You just never know a "foreign student" knocking at the front door of the house of someone who had never even seen me? Common so, I called them instead. Anne, Petit answered the phone. I introduced myself. I said I am John Akinyemi, a foreign student at Aurora College. "JOHN WHO"?, she asked. "JOHN AKINYEMI, I answered. Then I proceeded spelling my last name to her. I guess by this time she has given me the benefit of the doubt. Maybe this guy is legitimate. I told her that I had heard from the college that an African girl was living with her. I said I am trying to verify if, indeed she and her family were hosting this African girl?. I asked if she would not mind me stop by, introduce myself, etc. Five minutes is all that'd take to visit her", I added. "No problem". I showed up. She welcomed me into her home. There, I met Agnes. Anne Petit introduced me to her family: Peggy Petit her daughter, and John Pettit, her son. Both were teenagers at the time. The rest is history. Wait a minute, I take that back. Let us break down that word: HISTORY, into two component parts, namely "HIS" "STORY". From here forward, and as far as I am concerned writing Agnes's biography, I am dropping the "h" in "history" and substituting "m". In other words 1, from now on, it is "my" "story"! I promise you, I'll tell it as tellingly as I can. Trust me. I have a storyteller gene in my DNA!

Agnes had her elementary schooling at Machakos Girls Schooll. As that school name suggests, it is located appropriately at Machako's District in Kangundo is a location. It was a "girls school", which, by default means there is a separate Machakos Boys School. Machakos Girls School staff were mostly Europeans and Americans. It had very few African teachers. The same is true at Machakos Boys School, which Agnes's junior brother, Maingi attended. You can count the number of African teachers in one hand at either school. The "foreigners" lived in posh, manicured homes on campus. They had all the perks: gardeners, drivers, "house boys", in other words "cleaners", you name them. The "foreign teachers", enjoyed their paid vacation, namely, teach two years and get eighteen months paid vacation! What a deal! They might just as well be taking an African Safari all the time they were in Kenya.

The few African teachers were left to fend for themselves. They did not live on quarters. They commuted to work on their Raleigh bicycles (if they are lucky to have one). Students were required to wear uniforms. Machakos Girls School was located far away from Agnes's home. Because of this, Ndungwa, like all other students, stayed in the Boarding School during the school year. There, Agnes learned how to mend clothes, wash and iron her uniforms, sew with needle and thread. Lest, I forget: she learned how to cook and crochet too! She fondly remembered one of her teachers, Mrs Perry, whom she described as a fiersty little (starture-wise) English woman who smoked heavily but was very good and nurturing to the girls. Agnes relished how her parents NEVER missed showing up on campus for special school events. She recalled how "badly" she felt when her schoolmates did not have the pleasure of their parents' presence during such events. Agnes learned early in life to be a "comforter" to her unfortunate friends. She shared her good fortune of her parents' presence at such events by making sure she introduced her girlfriends to them. And ofcourse, her parents hugged, greeted them in the native languages, be that Kikamba, Kiswahili, or other tribal dialects.

Church attendance on Sundays was mandatory. Girls had to line up in a formation, military style, to march to the church, which was miles away from the Boarding School campus. One of the girls was in command. She usually stood the tallest, at the back of the fornation from where she would command "Right, left, right left forward march, stop; right-about turn". Agnes recalled her utter confusion when the order says "right about-turn, or "left-about-turn! She said to me, "I would turn right, turn left, see the confusion of the row of girls in the front of me, and utter confusion in the several back rows of the formation! She recalled, "I would just panick." I hated that command, she added.

Holiday life away from the Boarding School was a lot different and fun, she said to me, years later. Her chores included cooking and serving her siblings when it was her turn to do so. It is noteworthy to say that I, too, learned likewise when I was growing up in Nigeria. Agnes told me a story about one of her older brothers whose turn it was to "cook and serve" his siblings. He was taking longer than usual doing so; so Agnes's body language must have said to him "please hurry up; I'm hungry." The bother said to her: "Don't look at me like that. I am not your mother!"

A word about getting ready for special holiday celebrations. Five days before Christmas (which, by the way is Agnes's birthday) you have to wash and clean the floor, dust wooden furniture, iron the linen, change seat coverings to newly laundered, white coverings (in preparation for Easter Sunday, or bright yellow, which is the traditional color of the Kamba People to which Agnes and the family belonged, in preparation for celebration of Kenya Independebce Day, or mixture of red and green for Christmas) For Christmas she would help her siblings cook the festive meal, usually rice, chapati, nnama (AKA meat) vegetables consiting of fresh corn, beans. carrots, etc., Kenyans refer to this meal as "Ischio, or Irio", depending on which Tribe they belong. The Kamba People call it "ischio". Other tribes, I believe the Luos call it "irio." In addition, Agnes and her siblings would decorate the house with paper marche of different designs, and festive colors.

Getting ready for Celebrating Christmas.

Agnes and her Muthiani Family always looked forward to attending Christmas Service. She recalled, "This is the day you hear about the birth of a baby, born in the Manger because there was no room for Him in the inn. Christmas, she said, was always a day of great joy and rejoicing, adding, "a day to reflect and thank God. As early as she could remember, she recalled, "Christmas is a day we learned that "Baby Jesus is the Reason for the Season".

Getting ready for Celebrating Easter Sunday.

Agnes didn't share too much with me of her early childhood memories of Easter Celebration other than she and her siblings attended church on Easter Sunday. The church she attended was founded by the African Inland Mission. At home, through family devotion and reading of Scriptures, she had learned about Jesus's Crucifction and Resurrection It is noteworthy to state that our daughter, Adedoyin Akinyemi, did not like the Crucifiction story either. She was absolutely horrified that they forced a crown of thorns on Jesus's head, and nailed him to the Cross, spat on him, beat Him, called him all kinds of (filthy) names, and scorged Him, leaving him to bleed to death. She just couldn't fathom it! Agnes and I recall an incident when some White boys shouted an N word unto us as they drove their car past our Bel Air home "Why did they shout the "N-word Nigger" on us, she asked? I responded, "didn't people call Jesus names in the Bible?". She was 7 or 8 years old at the time. So, like mother, like daughter in this regard. I find this truly amazing, indeed!

In contrasting Easter Sunday to Christmas, though, Agnes reiterarted: "Christmas was a time for: singing carols, listening to "happy" Scripture readings on the birth of Baby Jesus, etc. She recalled how "different" Christmas is "celebrated" in her home country of Kenya, compared to how it is celebrated in the US. How so?, I asked. She said "not as "highly commercialized" in Kenya as it is in America.." Back home, she added, people cooked and shared meals. They dont "charge gifts they don't need and cannot afford on plastic cards". That's the difference! Go girl!

Agnes, as previously mentioned, was the 8th child In a family of 10. She had six brothers and three sisters not including herself.

From the oldest to the youngest, their names are: Kaluki Musau (nee Muthiani), Wilson Wambua Muthiani (AKA Mualimo, Kikamba word that means "teacher"), Joseph Mwatu Muthiani, the agriculturalist, Isaac (AKA Isaka), Fred Ndeti, (AKA Mulangida),

Sila, Sister Mutio Kioko, (nee Muthiani), Agnes (AKA Ndungwa Muthiani (nee Akinyemi), sister Kaswii, Muthiani, Jackson Maingi Muthiani, and Mutune Muthiani (AKA Kanyoro). Regretably, all her siblings, except Kaswii, had passed within three months after Agnes died!

Agnes was proud of her position as the 8th child in her family. I recall an incident. We were at Phillips Library at Aurora College. As always, we were "disciplined". We had a time to study. We had a time to "socialize". This particular event, though, we had been studying and had decided to take a 10 minute or so break. We drifted into many topics, about future plans etc.. I remember her saying to me: "whoever I marry must agree to have ten children with me." I said to her, matter-of- factly :"I guess that rules me out!" She laughed. I didn't

Agnes's father was Andrew Muthiani (AKA Endelea). Endelea was a prayer warrior. He was a hard worker and a good family provider. He got up very early in the morning and commuted to work in a town called Thika. He took public transportation called Matatu, which translates to commuter van. Because of the long commute, he stayed in Thika but came home on Fridays to spend weekends with the family. He did this for many years That meant running the home affairs and 10 children fell to Agnes's mother. Her mother's name was NDILILI. Before I digress, let me finish my story about Endelea. After his long commute to Thika, he got another job. On that job, he rose to an acclaimed position as a "local judge" in the Kangundo Community. He got that position because he was a man full of wisdom. He settled many cases, including dispute over ownership of lands, farms (AKA Shambas), inheritance, domestic disputes between husbands and wives, etc.

Now back to Agnes's mother, Ndilili. She belonged to the Kamba (AKA Kikamba) Tribe. All Muthianis belong to that tribe. Philogenetically, the KAMBA People belong to the Nilotic Group. Story has it that Ndilili just packed her belongings and migrated to Kangundo. There she met and found Endelea. Before too long, she became his wife! What a sweet deal! She raised all 10 children! Besides that humongous duty, and label as a "homemaker", she supervised family business..She prided herself in learning how to read the Bible, called Biblia in Kamba language to her children. She was also a good singer. She was very meticulous and tidy- freak.. I remember asking one of her great grandchildren to sweep off chicken "poopoo" from the outdoor area surrounding her outdoor kitchen floor. That's how meticulous she was.

She demanded and earned the respect of all in the community.. Story has it that she would keep gifts, such as clothing and bedsets we had sent her from America in her closet. She would not use them but whenever church members came to visit her and Endelea, she would show those presents to them and say "my daughter and son-in-law sent these to me from America!" When we visited her, we found out she had not worn the dresses, she had not used the bed linen, pillows, etc, that supposedly were hers to enjoy! Silverware was still in the shipping package. But proud she was to "show and tell" them that her children in America had sent them to her.

Agnes's paternal grandfather was Mwatu Wangoma. He was a "fierce" man of great valor. I am told he had many wives and children. Reportedly, he had served during the Israeli war. Story has it that he died in Kenya after the war fighting for one of his wives.

Agnes's grandmother was called Mikelli, which translates to "Michelle". One of Agnes"s nieces (Mikki) was named after her grandmother, Nau, Endelea's mother Mikeli (Michell) Mbithe. Story has it that the grandmother lived with Agnes's family until she passed. Agnes recalled many fond memories of her.

Ndungwa had two paternal uncles: Uncle Moses Ndolo, and Uncle Erastus Wambolu. Both were entrepreneurs. They traded in commercial goods and raised chicken in a modern day poultry by today's standards.. I recall an incident when we visited them with our children, Adedoyin and 'Tobi. It was in the morning. They had accompanied their cousins to pick up fresh- laid eggs from the poultry. That was the first time our kids saw eggs laid in a poultry ever! I remember this so well because at breakfast that morning, 'Tobi refused to eat eggs. His cousins asked why he would not eat eggs that had been freshly picked. "Why aren't you eating?" they asked him. He said "because I don't eat eggs that come from the chicken's poopoo". "Where do the eggs you eat in America come from? they asked? He replied "from Giant! I wonder what had gone on in his cousins' minds. Some strange evolution?

I recall visiting one of Agnes's aunts during my visit to Kenya. She gave me a hen, "kuku bird" she called her. This hen was raised as free roamer, which meant she was NOT cage-raised as is the case with modern poultry. Believe me, once you eat coiked free-roaming chickens, you will never want to eat cage-raised chickens!

Agnes was raised in a very religious family background. Let me paint for you a picture of what I mean. A typical day would start with family prayer, devotion, and reading of a Scripture. Each child would read a verse and hand over the Bible (AKA BIBLEA) to the next sibling, who, in turn would follow suite. The oldest sibling, was named Wilson WAMBUA MUTHIANI. Close family members called him "MUALIMO", which means "teacher", because he was trained as a teacher. Wambua was good as a "choirmaster"and Conductor of music also. He waves his hand in air and gestures them the way a Conductor does in a musical concert. At the sane time, he sings along with them in his baritone voice.

Each morning at family devotion, Wambua would start reading a chosen verse in the Scripture. Succeeding siblings followed suit in order, by age, until it was time for the youngest, named Mutune, (AKA Kanyoro). It is interesting to note that the oldest sibling was KALUKI MUSAU, (nee Muthiani); however, she and her husband, DANIEL MUSAU (AKA Danielli) maintained this same tradition in their own family unit. Therefore, they did not participate in this scenario. After reading the Scripture, the father, ENDELEA, prayed. Usually, he said a long prayer, thanking God for every provision. He thanked God for the maize or corn (AKA Bemba in Kamba language). He thanked God for cows and goats he raised. He thanked God for coffee, macadamia nuts, cassava, papaya, he grew in his shambas (AKA) his farms. He would then proceed to thanking God for his church members: he was not a pastor. He thanked God for his pastor all right. but after church service, church members would follow Endelea, including the pastor, to his home. Talkng about the Feast of the Tabernacle!

Now, more about his church members. I recall my very first visit to the family in Kenya. This was 14 years after Agnes and I had been married in Washington DC. I was "jubilating" at the experience of meeting my father-in-law. The flight from the Baltimore Washington International Airport.had taken a toll on me and Agnes. Subsequently, the jet lag I suffered required that I sleep late the first day in Kenya. My father-in-law had begun to wonder what kind of son-in-law he had gotten from NIGERIA:

Why is he still sleeping? It is past 10:00 am, local time and he is still sleeping? "what a lazy bump!, he probably said unto himself: "we work very hard in Kenya; we cannot afford to sleep all day! Suffice it to say I felt asleep during his morning family prayer. Mind you, it was postponed a couple hours to accommodate this sleepy son-in-law participating in this important ritual. I was gently knodged out of my sleep by Agnes. All I remember was my father-in-law saying "JESO KRISTO" to which I said Amen. It didn't take me too long to figure he had come to the end of the prayer by saying Jesu Christo (AKA Jesus Christ).

Another recollection was that the first Sunday after our arrival, my father-in-law had asked church members, family members and community well wishers to come "celebrate" the coming home of his son-in-law. Large tents had been erected. A big cow had been slaughtered, wives of family members were busy preparing dinner, etc.! Attendance was full. Prayer had been said. Choirs had begun to sing familiar hymns of praise. Now it was time for John Akinyemi to address the group. The only problem is I cannot speak to them in Kikamba language. A large group of them cannot speak or understand "American" English. I.summoned my brother-in-law, Jackson Maingi Muthiani, as my translator! My speech went well. I felt two things; first, I remember the Biblical story of the Prodigal Son. Only this time, I was being welcomed to my wife's native land by my father-in-law and secondly, I felt as if had been awarded a Nobel Peace Prize by my in-laws welcoming me into the family. They accepted me unconditionally. They showed me genuine love. Praise God!

Fast backwards:

Agnes left KENYA, at age 15, to seek high school education in the USA. Yes, you read it right: at age 15!. Up until this time she had lived a simple agrarian life in a small village in KANGUNDO. To her, Tala Market was the biggest local market. Contemplating traveling to the USA for higher education was a major life event to her. She had been fortunate to be selected, on a competitive basis, by the KENYA government as part of a program by the then USA President John Fitzgerald Kennedy (AKA JFK). That Program's goal was to "educate" students from the Third World countries, such as from Kenya, East Africa. It is noteworthy to state that the 46th President Barack Husein Obama's own father had come 2 years earlier than Agnes to the US under a similar program.

How in the world does a young 15-year old prepare for this once-in-a-lifetime opportunity, and, for that matter a life changing event? Several thoughts must have gone through Agnes's mind. "I never lived in NAIROBI, a big city, the capital of KENYA. How do I navigate my way to the Embassy of Kenya? How do I go to the US Embassy in Nairobi, the capital city of Kenya? How in the world am I going to go by the local transportation (AKA MATATU)?

Thanks be to God, Agnes, many years testified to me: "my brother-in-law, DANIELI MUSAU, provided the answer! He took me by his car to Nairobi to obtain the required paperwork such as application for US visa, make interview appointments after completion of Visa Application, and ultimately see me depart for the USA!

A year later, Danielli's oldest daughter, NDINDA MUSAU, Agnes's niece, followed suit However, she didn't come under JFK sponsored program. To this day, Agnes's younger brother, JACKSON MAINGI MUTHIANI, and nieces, KALEKJE MUSAU,

KATUNGE MUSAU, MUTHEO KAVUU, (nee MUSAU), and MBETE KNOLLS MUSAU credit their aunt, NDUNGWA, as their Pioneer, Mentor, and "MATRIACH",for their coming to America!

Agnes and I were "blessed" to "sponsor" my brother-in-law, JACKSON MAINGI MUTHIANI to come to the USA for college in 1972. Agnes had just graduated from Howard University with a Master of Science degree in Microbiology, and I, with a Doctorate degree. We figured it was time for us to "reach out and touch somebody else" and make life better, if we can." There's no loftier thing to do than provide college education for those who follow us. It is, however, noteworthy to say no matter how much and how well we wanted to provide a "better life" or, a "higher education" for someone we love. It is ultimately the "personal choice" that someone makes to "take the Barton and run the relay race with it. I am so glad MAINGI did just that. He came to Aurora in 1972, obtained a BA degree from AURORA UNIVERSITY four years later. And when he was leaving, he passed the Barton to his niece, Kalekje Musau, who attended Aurora College from 1976. She, in turn, passed the Barton to Katunge Musau, who also attended Aurora College. Maingi went on to obtain a Master's degree from Governor State University, Chicago, IL. He later held a high Management Position at KOBIL (AKA MOBIL Equivalent in Kenya). Both Kalekje and Katunge are in the field of Social Work in Illinois.

Upon arrival at the New York International Airport in 1961, Agnes's program required that she attends high school. Guess where? Mather School in Beaufort, S. Carolina! She traveled by Greyhound Bus to Beaufort. She had two years there. She then transferred to Madona (Catholic) High School in Aurora, Illinois. She graduated the summer of 1964. I met her the Fall of 1964. I was a Sophomore. She was a Freshman. I remember meeting her on August 24 of that year. We started out as "friends". We had similar courses in college. We were "disciplined". We knew we have a goal; to obtain our education. We were focused. In those days, there was no comingling or cohabitation in dormitories in those days. There were Memorial Hall for women, and Jenkin Hall and Wilkinson Hall for men. I stayed in the same room at Wilkinson Hall for men..

If you wanted to "visit" either of the dormitories or.pick up your date, the announcement in the PA system would say "Men on the Floor" followed by "rushing of feet or giggling of college girls on their floor. Agnes had a roommate, Cindy Blazier, a humble, brilliant lady from Elgin, IL. They stayed at Randal House, which apparently was sold to the college by a Chemistry Professor, Dr Wallie Hines. Agnes and Cindy remain long time friends until the day Agnes passed. It is noteworthy to state that Cindy (married to Robert Skelly,) has known her just as long as I have: since 1964) Fifty-seven years of great friendship ! What a blessing!

College life was a lot of fun. We were disciplined. We were focused. We knew we had come to America to get higher education. That was our number 1 priority We studied hard. We spent hours studying at the Phillips Library of Aurora College. Every spare moment, we were there at the library or Organic Chemistry laboratory performing experiments. We knew the opening and closing hours if both. In fact, unbeknownst to us, a Librarian at Phillips Library had noticed our constant visits, she made a remark "You guys are dedicated to studying.. I see you all the time here." "Thank you, we politely said to her. We were thirsty for education We had traveled thousands of miles from Africa for it That was

OUR GOAL! Besides that, we had a lot of treasured memories: of college life to include our favorite professors: Dr. Patrick McFarlane (AKA Dr Pat) and his wife, Mrs. Eleanor McFarlane (AKA Mrs. (Pat). The husband and wife were pretty much the professors at the Biology Department. In order to major in Biology, you had to have them..The McFarlanes were an institution at Aurora College. They taught John's first cousin, Samuel Soremekun, who completed four years of study in three years and graduated in1959. He later obtained an MD and specialized in Anaesthiology.

Besides study, Agnes and I enjoyed college life. We have many fond memories of attending "Winter Carnival". Winter Carnival was, (and I believe may still be) a social event. To attend a winter gala means a time to "dress to kill." It was the tradition in college in those days. Girls wore long black dresses. Their boy friends, (BF), wore dark suits, or a coat and tie. Cindy Skelly (nee Blazier), Agnes's long time friend and roommate for four years sewed a gorgeous navy blue long dress that Agnes wore to her first Winter Carnival. She looked gorgeous when I picked her up. I wore the only suit I had brought from Nigeria It was a well-tailored suit, made in Canada. My late Mother gave it to me when I left home for the USA on July, 1963 as a present.

Homecoming is another memorable social event. It is a time to meet classmates and reminisce over college days experiences. Agnes and I attended and enjoyed the 47th- year Aurora College Homecoming. However, she did not attend the 50 Year Homecoming because of her heath. She, however, persuaded me to attend, and represent her, nevertheless. So I did. I was asked to participate in a video session titled "Story Teller" and, I did. Here's the clip:

We still communicate with our old college friends, including Ralph Corson, Dan Dobbert, Cindy Skelly, and Craig Bailey. Ralph graduated in 1965, and married Azar. Ralph is retired. He and his wife live in Puerto Rico. All our other colleagues are retired as well.

Agnes worked part time in the college cafeteria. She always told me of Mrs. Mabry, and Mrs. Epperson. They were Supervisors making sure the Cafeteria served nutritious food three times a day. In those days, students "prepaid" when they registered for the school term if they lived in dormitories. It is incumbent upon them to show up in a line when the Cafeteria opens to serve meals. It was always good to see Agnes when she was scheduled to work there.

We took similar courses together in college. We sat side by side in science courses. For our laboratory courses, we operated next to each other when we performed experiments in Orgarnic Chemistry. We fondly remember Dr. Roehrig, our Organic Chemistry Professor. He challenged us. He made us solve all the problems in our text book of Organic Chemistry written by Morrison and Boyd.

Agnes participated in dramatic arts also. I remember watching her play the part of Tichuba in a play directed by Mr. Tracy, Assistant Professor of Dramatic Arts. She enjoyed painting as well. Her favorite Professor of Art was a lady named Mrs. Ruth VanSykel Ford. She lived in a house architecturally designed and completely submerged underground. The only clue you would have was the driveway leading to and from the area underground!

Other friends in college include Tom and his brother, Dan Dobbert, Margaret Franklin (nee Peters) from Panama, and Abid Dagfall, from Lebanon. Abid and his wife, Hala were very gracious and kind to Agnes one summer. They hosted Agnes at their "married" students quarters. Agnes remembers this so well. Decades later she told her Lebanon-born doctor, Dr. Moussawi, a Psychiatrist who specialized in the treatment of dementia, about Abid Dagfall! It is amazing people remember how well you treat them!

Margaret Franklin was traumatized when she learned of Agnes's passing. She had met Agnes the summer of 1968. She wondered if her friend had had a happy married life. I assured her Agnes did. She called a few more times, asking me for clarifications. Apparently she was working on completing a project. It sounded to me as "register" of some kind and she wanted to make sure she had the correct facts for the project.

After college, Agnes attended the Copley Memorial Hospital, Aurora, Illinois, where she trained as a Medical Technologist. She passed her medical technology registration exam and earned the designation of the American Society of Clinical Pathology, (ASCP). She rented a room close by. I remember her landlord, Mr. Krinner, an immigrant from Eastern Europe who owned and lived downstairs and rented the upstairs apartment to Agnes.

Agnes got a Medical Technologist position at the Massachussetts General Hospital. Which means she had to relocate to Boston, MA. She shared an apartment with two women. To this date, I remember her address there. It was 1118 Massachusetts Ave., Boston. MA. I remember her telephone, too, I think I called her morning, day, and night as if she was my medicine!

Post Graduate School:

After Aurora College, I went to, and obtained a Master of Science (MS) Degree from Northern Illinois University, (NIU), DeKalb, IL While there I shared a 3- bedroom apartment with two other graduate students. They were from Pakistan and Iran. There I met a young lady, Sharon Mona Lynn (nee McClean). Sharon invited me to her wedding in Peoria, IL in 1968. We lost contact. She and her first husband had moved to Canada. Fifty years later, we reconnected!

We are still friends today! While at NIU, I supported myself working nights on call whenever someone didn't show up. That meant driving to Armour Dial, a company that manufactures Dial soap. That worked well. Which meant I would be back to my class before 9:00 am.

While at Howard University. we lived at 1451 Park Road, NW, Washington DC until one day, upon return from school, we found our 5th floor apartment had been robbed! An inside job we suspected. We called and filed Police Report, but nothing matured. We moved out into another apartment, 1408 Kanawa Rd in Hyattsville. MD.

Our next adventure took us to the National Institutes of Health (NIH), Bethesda, MD. Agnes and I covered the midnight shift working in the Clinical Pathology Department under Dr. McLowry, MD. Agnes and I worked on "stats" which meant identifying bacteria and parasites from patients' specimens, such as blood, urine, spinal taps,.stool, saliva, etc., and reporting findings to the MD. This was year 1971. The year we got married! Our marriage was very small. Just three of us, namely, Agnes, I, and the person who pronounced us husband and wife. That person was a friend of my first cousin, Dr. 'Fola Soremekun. Both had become friends while Cousin Fola was working on his PhD in Afro-American history at the renowned Northwestern University, Evanston, Illinois. We went to work at NIH the night we were married!

At NIH, we made friends with Dr. Zierdt, a Research Scientist, and Esther C Williams, a Medical Technologist, who ended up retiring from the government after more than 40 years. We are still friends today with Esther, a friendship that so far has lasted the entire time Agnes and I had been married: 50 years! Praise God.

After NIH, Agnes worked for Lytton Bionetics as a Microbiologist. From there, she worked for the University of Maryland as a Medical Technologist. There she met, worked with, and became lifelong friend with Nancy Johns and her twin sister, Shirley Johns.

While at the University of MD, Agnes got a fellowship under the "Other Race' Program to study for her PhD. She completed her research. She began and almost completed her PhD dissertation when a rift happened between her and her major advisor. That was a down moment of her life. She told me when I picked her up. I remember telling her "this is not the end of life, because, as I remember telling her "when one door closes, another opens, and most of the time, the opened door offers bigger opportunities!" That's precisely what happened. Years later, Agnes got a job with the Department of the Army, at Aberdeen Proving Ground, (APG). MD.

FIRST DAY AT APG

First, Agnes had to report to the Civilian Personnel Office (CPO), which is located 12 or so miles a way, at Aberdeen, MD. The CPO in turn instructed her where to report: APG, Edgewood, Area MD That day, a young, 22 year-old African American lady, Teresa Dorman also reported to the CPO for similar instructions. Both she and Agnes were assigned to the same Directorate! That 22-year old, Teresa Dorman had mistakenly locked her car key inside her car. She got help retrieving her keys and raced to the Edgewood Area, where her workstation was located. She gave Agnes a ride. When she and Agnes arrived, they were surprised that the folks in Edgewood Area were in no rush at all! She wondered and later reflected if she had known she wouldn't have rushed from the CPO in Aberdeen to Edgewood. You never get a second chance to make that first impression. She and Agnes did not want to start their new job by reporting "late".

Agnes worked for, and retired from APG with 25 years of Government Service. Teresa worked for 32 or so years before she retired. They were longtime friends and confidante until Agnes passed away on June 2021.

Agnes photo as a scientist.

RETIREMENT

Getting ready for retirement is a "Personal Decision". There is no "one size fits all" regarding when to retire. She had done her homework. She availed herself of briefings from the CPO. They had provided her ALL the facts. I did the same thing with the United States Marine Corps, (USMC). Agnes retired from the US Army at the end of July 2006. I retired on September 30, 2006. At retirement, Agnes got numerous awards and citations. So did I. We thank God for that.

The US Office of Personnel Management, (OPM), handles all matters regarding Federal employees. They provided very useful information on retirement benefits, life insurance, health insurance, etc. Armed with to that information, I decided to MAINTAIN MY FEDERAL BLUE CROSS/BLUE SHIELD (BC/BS) Health coverage to include Agnes. Unbeknownst to me, I had chosen BC/BS health insurance for both of us when we started our careers with the Government. That was in 1981. In 1993, I left my old job at the US Army, Aberdeen Proving Ground, (USAPG). I was promoted to a new job, at the United States Marine Corps (USMC).

The Honorable C.A. Dutch Ruppersberger
2nd Congressional District
Maryland

Certificate of Special Recognition

Presented to

AGNES N. AKINYEMI

With Appreciation for Your Service and Achievement

IN RECOGNITION OF YOUR RETIREMENT FROM FEDERAL CIVILIAN SERVICE WITH 24 YEARS, 2 MONTHS OF DEDICATED SERVICE

July 31, 2006
DATE

MEMBER OF CONGRESS
2nd DISTRICT, MARYLAND

Agnes citations at her retirement ceremony.

After retirement, we maintained an active lifestyle. We both knew NOT to live a sedentary life after retirement. In fact, we did and enjoyed more physical activities. We spent time with our grandchildren, Isaiah, who was born on March 2006, and Joshua, who was born on June 2009. Isaiah literally spent his first two years with us. Both grandchildren relish their grandparents attending their many school activities: Parents-Teachers Association (PTA) meetings, Christmas concerts, sports activities, etc. They still relish grandma's cooking for them their favorite meals (Chinese fried rice, jollof rice, macaroni and cheese, chapati, etc) They remember grandma and grandpa planting a flower garden at their own house at Ellicott City, MD. They remember cookouts in summer. They remember grandma and grandpa shopping with them. They remember us to never miss celebrating birthdays with them. When the weather is nice they always challenged thir grandma to play soccer with them or run with them. For many years, Agnes always quoted them saying to her: "come on grandma, run!" They even challenged their grandma to playing basketball. I remember an incident. One day Joshua, (who was 7 or 8 years old at the time), was asked by another parent "what does your grandpa do for a living? He replied: "my grandpa puts one thing in the ground and makes it grow! That was a beautiful testimony to my hobby, gardening. Agnes shared the passion for gardening also. She claimed she had been gardening ever since she was a little girl. Her family assigned her a designated portion of land. It was for her to cultivate. The same was true for each of her siblings in Kenya. Agnes told me she used to climb mango trees as a little girl. She used to.serve as a Shepard bringing her family's herd of cattle home. I can attest to that. I saw her take a piece of stick, run after a cow that had left the pasture and brought that cow to the barn. We were visiting the family.st the time. Needless to say, I was impressed.

'Doyin and 'Tobi recall the many weekend mini vacations the family took them when they were growing up. My skin still cringes to this day when 'Doyin decided to swim deep water at Ocean City, a popular vacation in Maryland, near, New Jersey. She was so confident of her swimming ability, but Agnes and I were scared to death. She also scared the living life out of us when 'Doyin walked the hallway to a different hotel room door in a motel we had stayed! She and 'Tobi fondly recall our taking them to the White House, Museum of African History, the Washington Monument, and many culturally enriching "touring sites". Their childhood included memories of mini vacation to Hershey Park, Kings Dominion, etc.

Besides hobby, Agnes enjoyed music tremendously. She enjoyed. dancing. She did it all: danced to: highlife music from Nigeria and, Ghana. She loved to dance and sing along to the lyrics of Bob Marley, of Jamaica.,etc. She absolutely loved to listen to the Mormon Tabernacle Choir,. Her other favorites include the Handel Messiah, the tenor voices of Domingo Pavarotti, Andrea Bocelli, etc. Whenever I wanted Agnes to dance at home, all I had to do is "entertain" her by playing my CDs, particularly music of Fela Anikulapo Kuti. Chief Commander Sunny Ade and Missa Luba, an Afrjcan Mass Kenyan Folk Melodies. Agnes knew how to dance fox- trot, twist, and waltz. We did all that at Aurora College's social events I alluded to earlier.

Apart from hobbies, Agnes surrounded herself with good people. The good people included: all members in the extended family: clan, meaning the Soremekuns, the Akinyemis, the Muthianis, and the Musaus. They, in turn "adored" her. The coloquall expression "love her to death" is most apt to describe their affection. Upon learning of her death, they gave their testimonies and recalled how much they missed Agnes. I have included some, but certainly not all of these testimonies. They were too numerous to include in this biography. For this, I apologize. Suffice it to say that on behalf of Agnes, I thank each and everyone for their condolences, show of love and kindness during this difficult process of Grieving over our loved one.

However, I will be remisced if I didn't mention some people who played significant roles in the last four or five years of Agnes's life. By this I mean her Healthcare Providers. They include Dr. David Madder, DO, an Internal Medicine Specialist. Dr. Madder is our Primary Care Doctor. Mrs. Linda Bame, CHNP, is our Nurse Practitioner. Both of them work at the John's Hopkins University Hospital located at the White Marsh Community Center, White Marsh, MD. Agnes loved to wear hats, year long: Winter, Fall, Spring, or Summer. Dr. Madder noticed that. "I like your hat" he always said to her. Ofcourse, Agnes always replied "thank you". At the end of every office visit, Agnes always said to Dr. Madder a few French and Kiswahili greetings to show her appreciation for his medical care. Both Dr. Madder and Ms. Bame, CHNP, treated us with utmost care and attention to details..They "listened"to us. By this I mean their eyes locked with ours every time we visited them. We always sensed that they did so because nothing else was more important to them than to listen to us.. They did so with laser-focussed attention to details. They explained to us every detail of the medicines Agnes was taking. Because Agnes was on many medications, they explained possible interactions and the need to adjust the dose as these complications arise. I learned a lot from them. I learned to listen with rapt attention to details. I learned to keep a record of Agnes's vitals, such as her body temperature, her body weigh, her blood pressure, her urine volume, as well as being vigilant to note the color of her urine, and the consistency of her stool (color and whether the stool is "hard or soft)". It is noteworthy to mention that Agnes had "excellent" health until she turned 72. Her health began to decline after that. She had atrial fibrillation (AFIB). She took "Baby" aspirin as a preventative daily. She took Eliquis She was diagnosed with advanced stage Althymers Disease also. However, the primary cause of death was due to cardiac failure.

Taking care of Agnes during her battle with Dementia.

Seven Decades of Agnes's Life

William Shakespeare in As You Like It wrote, "there are Seven Stages of Man." At first the infant,.....

First Decade (1944 to 1954)

I did not know Agnes when she was an infant; however, I would, like Pope Paul ceremonially" kiss the soil" of Kangundo, Kenya, which Agnes walked on from infancy until she came to America at age 15. I would walk on the red soil of Kangundo, visit the site of Machakos Girls School, which laid the foundation of Agnes's life. At that school, Agnes learned many hymns and "Songs of worship" by memory.. She literally memorized the title and first verse of most hymns. All I had to say to her is the title of a hymn. For example, if I say to her 'All Things Bright and Beautiful", she would sing the whole hymn from memory. I would join her. The only difference is I would do so after I have opened my Methodist Hymnal! Before you know it, she and I are having our own "church service". We had so much fun doing this. This amazing memory of things learned in early years remains indelible during her battle with dementia during her 7th decade.

Second Decade (1954 to 1964)

This was a decade in which Agnes was suddenly transformed from living a "sheltered life" to making important life- changing decisions. During much of this decade, she had been surrounded by her siblings, family, friends and loved ones in her native home, Kenya.. During this decade, Agnes had to learn very quickly and grow fast to survive in a culture that was very different to what she had known: a culture in which "American English", that is, the way an American speaks English Language) was strange and unfamiliar to her. Mind you, up until this time, she had limited knowledge of "kings" English and grammar. Additionally, when she arrived at the JFK Airport in New York, she didn't have the luxury of being welcomed by any family member or close friend. At the end of the day, there was no father, no mother to run home to share the day's events! How many 15-tear olds can do that?, let alone do that in a different or "strange" culture? Let me tell you what I mean, by way of short story: We told our daughter one day: "you know your mother came to this country, USA at age 15, right? "Right Dad".I continued "we, (your mother and I) are willing to pay your way to any high school or college if, like your mother, you are willing to do likewise:. "What do you mean? she asked. Like for example, study in far away countries like France, Germany, or Italy? She said "I ain't going nowhere!

During this second decade, Agnes learned how to "survive" in America;. She learned how to set a goal: she learned how to focus on the goal she had established for herself; namely, to pursue education in America. She learned how to keep on going even when ithe going is rough. She told me this story: one summer, she was hired to clean after a White family in Chiquata, New York. She used the old-fashioned washing machine. She ironed clothes: socks, underwear and all for them. This family consisted of sjx adults and their first cousins. They "bandeded together to rent this resort home. They couldn't afford to pay much to Agnes. It was a menial job. It was exhausting because Agnes did this nonstop.Agnes was lucky when they gave her sardine, which was their left-over meal. Agnes told me one day that summer, she picked a hamburger someone had thrown into a garbage can!. During this decade, Agnes learned to persist,. She learned to persevere!. She learned to be resourceful She learned to never give up even when the going is rough. This reminds me of the late Pastor, Dr. George Schuller of Christal Cathedral, Orange County, California, who said, "Tough tines Don't Last, but Tough People Do."

It was during this decade that I met Agnes.. We started out first as "casual friends", I say that because I was dating my "girlfriend, 'Tayo, whom I had met at the School of Agriculure, Akure, Nigeria. She was given scholarship, with all expenses paid.. On top of that, full salary and stipend from the Government of Nigeria. From get go, this young lady wanted me to become a Jehovas Witness (JW). I politely refused. I told her "I respect your religion, but I cannot knock peoples' doors, and interpret the Bible to them the way a JW does. In other words I don't want to "proselytize" them. She was so adamant she could change me. but I knew better.. I didn't hide this story from Agnes. As a matter-of-fact when this young lady visited me one summer, for a few days at Aurora, she stayed with the American family that hosted Agnes at Aurora. In those days, there was no "hanky panky"anywhere on college campus, period. That colloquial means "no smooching" in today's language. I recall the College Dean of Men ordered a couple to distance themselves. "Why, you ask? they had been dancing too closely to each other on the dance floor during a Winter Carnival. Anyways, when this young lady, my "former" girlfriend returned to Nigeria after obtaining a Master's Degree from the University of New Hampshire, story has it that she ended up marrying a JW. I don't envy her or her spouse. To this day, I believe in marriage from and to someone with the same "yolk". To continue my story, my casual friendship with Agnes "developed" into "boy friend and "girlfriend". Like she, I was focused on my number 1 goal, which was education. After all, like she, I left my home country, Nigeria, several thousand of miles away to study in the USA. It is noteworthy to say that Agnes also had a boyfriend at the time. I didn't meet him, but she told me about him. That's how "open" we were! He was a young man from Tanzania, East Africa.. His name was Mwindashi Siamuitsa. He studied at Bowdoin College, more-or-less regarded by many, as "Baby" College of Boston or Harvard University in Boston, Massachusetts. Somehow, that relationship ended after a year or so. I don't know what he majored in. Agnes never heard from him ever since. It would be mist unkind iof me to say "good riddance" Instead, I say his loss is my gain.

To this date, I marvel at how, by the middle towards the end of each decade, I have observed a "divine" purpose in Agnes's brief seven decades of life. Let me explain. There is a popular saying: "morning shows the day". It bears repeating, if only to illustrate a point I am making: and that point is this. At 15, Agnes left Kenya to pursue higher learning. She did so brilliantly, but did not know for sure that God, the Divine, was preparing her for greater things to come. Then came Middle School, followed by high school. Then came College graduation in 1968. That to me, is a "divine plan". God's way of transitioning her to the second decade!

Third Decade (1964 to 1974)

During this decade, Agnes and I got married on August 1971. Both of us had graduated from Aurora University one year apart: I, in 1967, and she, in 1968. We figured we had accomplished our first goal of getting our first degrees, respectively. As I had alluded to earlier, we were constantly aware that we left Africa to obtain our higher education in America. Bravo. Mission accomplished! We figured now we can set another goal. Family planning. During this decade, our older child, Adedoyin Akinyemi, was born, on October 1974. She was, and remains a beauty to this date!

Our son, Olutobi Akinyemi, was born exactly a year minus a day apart, on October 1975. It is noteworthy to say our son-in-law, Randy Skipper (AKA Skip), was born on July 1971, a month before our wedding day! Skip celebrated his big "five- oh" as I write this biography! We are very "close" with our children. They are (and still remain) a part of our lives. During their earlier growing years, we literally had many "mini vacations" on weekends, especially when soccer practice or soccer games were not scheduled! 'Doyin was a choir member at the Oak Grove Baptist Church in Bel Air, MD. We were proud to see her participate in The Living Christmas Tree Choir presentations! 'Tobi made his parents an "instant VIP" in the Bel Air community after he singularly recited performance at his Middle School Christmas Concert in front of a packed audience and got a standing ovation! We were flattered every time we were out running some errands when people said to us "are you the parents of this beautiful boy who whaohed us at that Christmas performance"? Yes, we are, pointing to 'Tobi and saying to them" this is 'Tobi. It's such a joy when things like that happen. It's a "win-win" situation: the child feels he is recognized for an accomplishment and the parents feel great!

Fourth Decade (1974 to 1984)

I think I may be ahead of myself in counting the years that form a decadeI, or I better go back to my Primary School to learn how to count! Don't laugh. It is daunting for an 80 year-old to be sure the first 10 years of someone born in 1944 ae from 1944 to 1954. My challenge is to keep this straight on my mind. It gets muddy sometimes! Trust me!

Fifth Decade (1984 to 1994)

My daughter graduated from the C. Milton Wright High School, Bel Air in 1984. She remembered her mother could not and did not attend her graduation because my father-in-law had passed in Kenya, East Africa, and she and I decided Agnes would fly to Kenya for her father's burial while I attend 'Doyin's graduation. Fair deal, right? Nevertheless, 'Doyin remembered her mother's "absence"! The family moved from our first house in Baltimore to Bel Air in 1981. Agnes and I decided to move closer to our first government jobs at the Aberdeen Proving Ground, MD. Agnes retired from the Department of the Army (DA) after serving 25 years (1981 to 2006). I spent one-half of my Federal Government career (1981 to 1993) with the DA, and the other half working for the United States Marine Corps at their Headquarters in Arlington, VA

Sixth Decade (1984 to 1994). This is a decade

During this decade

Seventh Decade (2004 to 2014)

During this decade, I am convinced God was still in charge, orchestrating what was meant to be a prelude to His grand finale! HE was preparing me to be of strong faith. HE was reminding me of the wedding vow, we had made to each other on August, 1971. "I, John Ayoola Akinyemi take this woman, Agnes Ndungwa Akinyemii to be my wife: to love her "for better for worse, in health and sickness, etc.

This decade, and the "added" blessing of additional 6 years, witnessed our true demonstration of that wedding vow. I am ABSOLUTELY CERTAIN that Agnes would have taken good care of me if the shoes were turned around! She was an amazing woman: a one-of-a-kind! I feel so blessed to have shared 57 years of her life (2021 minus year 1964, when we first met). We gave lived an incredible life together! I couldn't have written this incredible story! She was my "better half". She made me a better person, a better husband, and a better father to our two "adult children". She nade me a better grandfather to our grandchildren, Isaiah and Joshua, and their brothers, Randy Skipper II, and Malik Skipper. This time period made us appreciate one another. This time period made us realize how short life is, even as Agnes lived to her mid 70s. She passed at age 76! We will for ever remember her. We will hold dear to memories of her. We will remember the legacies she had passed unto us. She was a consumate wife and lifetime partner. We were inseparable in the sense that I couldn't have written her story without touching my story. We loved each other. Her joys were my joys. Her sorrows were my sorrows. I recall very vividly, a down moment when her PhD Advisor turned her down after completing and defending her PhD dissertation at the University of MD.

As previously mentioned, I picked her up, that day. I listened to her story, of how she was let down. I shared her feeling of absolutely being "rejected and disappointed. And then I told her," this is not the end of life; when one door closes, God opens another door. That door reveals greater opportunities.

Agnes went on to archive greater opportunities alright She ended up heading a laboratory working for the Government and ultimately retiring from, a Research Laboratory of the Department of the Army, at the Aberdeen Proving Gtound, MD, after 24 years of service, (from 1982 to July 2006).

Thus, her Seventh Decade (2104 to 2014) was blessed with additional 6 years, (2014 to June 2021, the day God called her to rest.

On the following day after she had passed. On June 16, Skip, 'Doyin, and I met with the Funeral Director, Steve. We went over the details. Within the first hour or so of our meeting, Steve said to us "Ms Agnes is here now. They had picked her body from the Hospital. We set the funeral day to on the following day, which was exactly one week after her death It is noteworthy to state that several years earlier, Agnes and I had bought a family plot whuch could accommodate the four of us in the family, namely her, myself, and our two "adult children" when that day comes. As I look back to that decision I thank God for it. We had our Will. We had pre-paid everything, EXCEPT, for the funeral. I had earlier believed that burial and funeral cost items were NOT the same. They were separate and distinct cost items. So, during our meeting, Steve explained everything to us in detail. He helped us "navigate" our options going forward. We saw many caskets online. We chose the.one most befitting. I paid for it right there and then. Next, we talked about other items. We set the Funeral for the following day. Many Family members, friends, and well-wishers attended. The list included, most but not neccesarily everyone who attended. For this, I apologize. I contend with that battle of selection, as previously alluded to in this biography. it to say that our neighbors, Abel Rebolla, neighbor to the left of us. and Ken, and his wife, to the right of our house, had attended. Our previous neighbor from Bel Air, Fran Wirth, did as well. Fran gave an eulogy, a beautiful testimony of how she remembered Agnes. Our long-term friends, Karen Henderson, Margaret Perry, her other daughter, (who worked at the John's Hopkins Hospital) also attended. Mr. Kehinde Talabi, our relative from Nigeria, attended. Kehinde served as one of the pallbearers. Other pallbearers included Skip, our son-in-law and our grandchildren. Agnes's nieces, Kakekje Musau, Katunge Musau, and Mutheu Kavuu and nephew, Maingi Musau and his lovely wife, Jane attended with their family members. Our sister-in-law, Salome Muthiani and her three daughters, Mikki Muthiani, Mirabelle (AKA Mira) Muthiani came also to the funeral. Mikki brought her son, Maingi Junior, with her from Atlanta. My first cousin, Dr. Maurice Adekunle Soremekun, MD, and his lovely wife, Dr. Bessie Soremekun, PhD, attended. Her husband, gave an eulogy. Unfortunately, my immediate Akinyemi Family members, and.my maternal aunt, Mrs. Mary Soremekun, and her daughter, my first cousin, Ms. Iyabo Soremekun, who both live in Miami, Florida could not attend, largely because of time to arrange fir someone to take care of my aunt, who will soon turn 94 on her birthday! Praise God. However, we did receive telephone calls, text messages, and email from virtually everywhere, from Kenya, Nigeria, South Africa, and all over the United Kingdom, where our families are scattered. On behalf of the entire Families of Akinyemi, monetary gifts and living tree donated by my First Cousin and his wife, the Soremekuns and my next-door neighbor, Ken and his wife to be planted in National Parks across the Country. Soremekun, Muthiani, and Musau, I thank you all for your kind thoughts, prayers, condolences, and encouragement fduring this difficult time of our loss. I am eternally grateful for, and to, you.

PHOTOS

John's father, the Late Joseph M. Akinyemi, 1951 to 1956. He died too soon at age 51.

My first cousins and my older sister at center.

Our traditional African outfit photo is shown.

Agnes Akinyemi relaxes at Bel Air MD

Preventative medicine, due diligence to personal health, balanced diet, daily exercise regimen will, in my view...

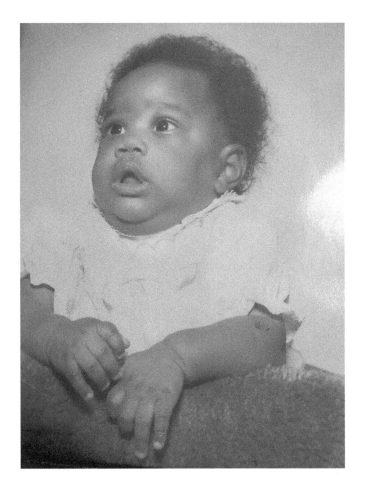

Photo of Adedoyin Akinyemi, our older child is shown here.

At the funeral: standing left to right: Salome, Randy, Skipper, Adedoyin Akinyemi and John Akinyemi.

Wedding photos (English traditional and African native attires).

Agnes and John Akinyemi sent this photo as our Christmas
greeting card to friends and family members.

Agnes is shown by herself wearing her native attire.

Daughter's BS Nursing degree graduation from the University
of Maryland.

Standing left to right: Olutobi Akinyemi, Adedoyin Akinyemi, and John Akinyemi.

Agnes's mother.

Our wedding, August 1971.

Muthiani's BA graduation: Left to right: Mutheo Muthiani, Mikki, John, Agnes, Mira Muthiani, Salome Muthiani and Jackson Maingi that appear Muthiani.

Agnes Akinyemi and John Akinyemi.

Standing left to right: Agnes Akinyemi,
Randy Skipper, and Adedoyin Akinyemi.

Fifi and Agnes Akinyemi.

John's first cousins and older sister at the center.

Agnes and I dancing to celebrate her Hospital discharge in 2018.

Agnes at home in Rosedale, Maryland enjoying the fire pit.

John Akinyemi and Agnes Akinyemi at the Marine Corps Birthday Celebration, 2024-2025, or thereabout.

Standing left to right: Maingi Muthiani, Agnes and John Akinyemi, taken at grand nephew's wedding.

From left to right Mikki Muthiani, Agnes's niece (her face is partly shown), myself and my first cousin, Iyabo Soremekun, (far right). This picture was taken to celebrate my Aunt's 90th birthday in Florida.

John's mother, Marion F. Akinyemi, and Agnes' father, Andelea Muthiani and mother, Ndilili Muthiani. This photo was taken when John's mother travelled to Kenya to meet Agnes' parents.

Wedding picture of Ndeti Muthiani, one of Agnes' six brothers.
This picture was taken in the 1960s.

CPSIA information can be obtained
at www.ICGtesting.com
Printed in the USA
LVHW071743060722
722845LV00010B/277